REMARKABLE PEOPLE

Kristen Stewart

by Anita Yasuda

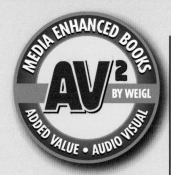

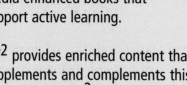

AV² by Weigl brings you media enhanced books that support active learning.

AV² provides enriched content that supplements and complements this book. Weigl's AV² books strive to create inspired learning and engage young minds for a total learning experience.

Go to **www.av2books.com**, and enter this book's unique code. You will have access to video, audio, web links, quizzes, a slide show, and activities.

BOOK CODE

G 2 6 1 8 5

Audio
Listen to sections of the book read aloud.

Video
Watch informative video clips.

Web Link
Find research sites and play interactive games.

Try This!
Complete activities and hands-on experiments.

Due to the dynamic nature of the Internet, some of the URLs and activities provided as part of AV² by Weigl may have changed or ceased to exist. AV² by Weigl accepts no responsibility for any such changes. All media enhanced books are regularly monitored to update addresses and sites in a timely manner. Contact AV² by Weigl at 1-866-649-3445 or av2books@weigl.com with any questions, comments, or feedback.

Published by AV² by Weigl
350 5th Avenue, 59th Floor
New York, NY 10118

www.av2books.com   www.weigl.com

Library of Congress Cataloging-in-Publication Data

Yasuda, Anita.
 Kristen Stewart / Anita Yasuda.
    p. cm. -- (Remarkable people)
 Includes index.
 ISBN 978-1-61690-163-9 (hardcover : alk. paper) -- ISBN 978-1-61690-164-6 (softcover : alk. paper) -- ISBN 978-1-61690-165-3 (e-book)
 1. Stewart, Kristen, 1990- Juvenile literature. 2. Actors--United States--Biography--Juvenile literature. I. Title.
 PN2287.S685Y37 2010
 791.4302'8092--dc22
 [B]
                              2010006159

Printed in the United States in North Mankato, Minnesota
1 2 3 4 5 6 7 8 9 0   14 13 12 11 10

052010
WEP264000

Editor: Heather Kissock
Design: Terry Paulhus

Photograph Credits
Weigl acknowledges Getty Images as the primary image supplier for this title.

Every reasonable effort has been made to trace ownership and to obtain permission to reprint copyright material. The publishers would be pleased to have any errors or omissions brought to their attention so that they may be corrected in subsequent printings.

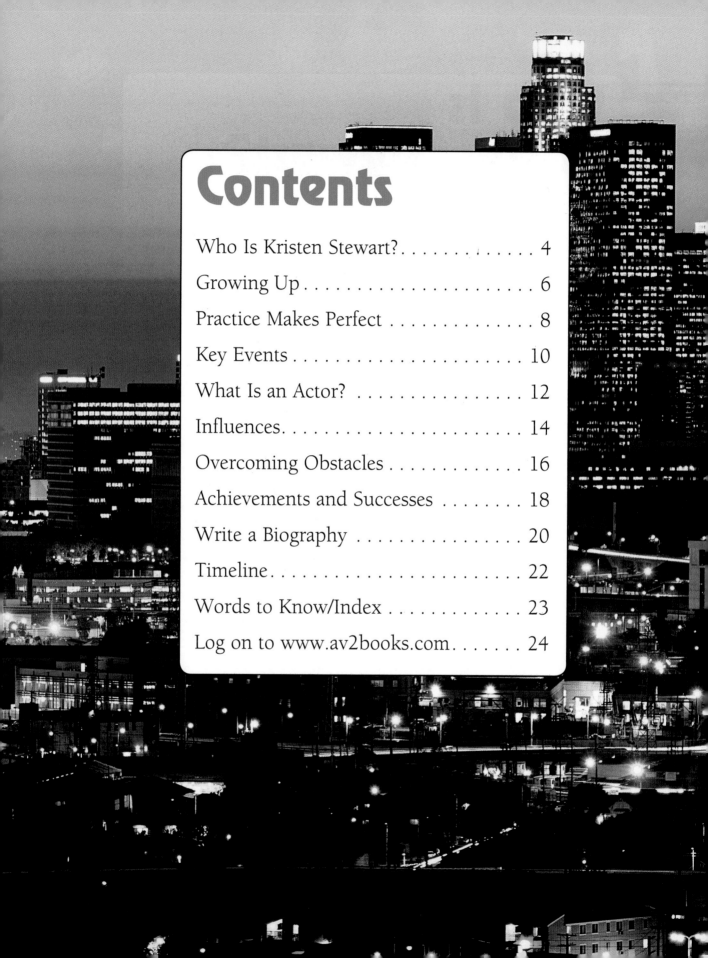

Contents

Who Is Kristen Stewart?

Thanks to the Twilight movies, Kristen Stewart has become well known around the world. Playing the role of Bella Swan has given her the opportunity to showcase her acting skills to a worldwide audience. She is now in demand for roles in other major motion pictures.

Kristen has been a **professional** actor since the age of eight. Her first role was a non-speaking part in a Disney Channel movie called *Thirteenth Year*. This was followed by a speaking role in *The Safety of Objects*, in which she co-starred alongside Patricia Clarkson. Kristen's first big break, however, came in 2002, when she played Jodie Foster's daughter in *Panic Room*. These early appearances earned Kristen praise and led to her being cast in *Twilight*.

"I like being in movies that have a great story. I'm not so interested in being a Hollywood star. It's a job, you know. When you wake up at six in the morning every day for a week, it feels like hard work."

The role of Bella Swan in the Twilight movies has brought Kristen a great deal of attention. Her face has appeared on many magazine covers, including *Teen Vogue*. In 2009, she won the Teen Choice Movie award for best actress in a drama. Her competition for this award included Angelina Jolie and Nicole Kidman.

Growing Up

Kristen Jaymes Stewart was born on April 9, 1990, in Los Angeles, California. While still young, her family moved to Colorado for a few years before returning to Los Angeles, where they have lived ever since. Kristen's father, John, is a television **producer**. Her mother, Jules, is a **script supervisor**. Kristen has three brothers, Cameron, Dana, and Taylor.

In her free time, Kristen enjoys playing sports with her brothers and getting together with friends. Many of Kristen's friends have been in her life since kindergarten. When she began acting, they were supportive and did not let it impact on their friendship.

Kristen attended public school until the seventh grade. Once she began appearing in more movies, Kristen found it a challenge to work and attend regular school. She began studying online, with Laurel Springs School. The school suited Kristen's demanding schedule.

■ The Stewarts live in Woodland Hills, which is part of the greater Los Angeles area.

Get to Know California

Mammal
Grizzly Bear

Flower
California Poppy

Tree
Redwood

OREGON
IDAHO
WYOMING
NEVADA
UTAH
CALIFORNIA
COLORADO
ARIZONA
NEW MEXICO

Pacific Ocean

0   500 Miles
0   500 Kilometers

Sacramento is the capital of California. Los Angeles is the state's largest city.

Nestor Studio was Hollywood's first movie studio. It opened in 1911. By 1915, most films made in the United States were being produced in the Los Angeles area.

Death Valley is the lowest point in California. It is 282 feet (86 meters) below sea level.

The first motion picture theater opened in Los Angeles on April 2, 1902.

Grauman's Chinese Theatre in Los Angeles is known for the hand and footprints of Hollywood stars on the sidewalk outside. The tradition began in 1927 with actors Mary Pickford and Douglas Fairbanks.

Kristen grew up in a city known for its connection to the movie business. How do you think living there influenced the choices Kristen has made in her life?

Practice Makes Perfect

Kristen did not plan on becoming an actor. An **agent** from the Gersh agency attended her school's Christmas concert. He saw a special talent in Kristen's performance, even though she was only eight years old. Her parents were uncertain about their daughter pursuing an acting career. However, Kristen was determined to become an actor. Over time, her parents supported her choice.

Kristen received no formal training to be an actor. She learned on the job.

Kristen signed with the Gersh Agency. Shortly after signing with her agency, Kristen landed her first television role. It was in a Disney Channel movie called *Thirteenth Year*. Many **auditions** later, she got the part of Sam in *The Safety of Objects*. When Kristen was only 12 years old, she was cast in *Panic Room*. Kristen's performance was nominated for a Young Artist award.

QUICK FACTS

- Kristen has three dogs, Oz, Jack, and Lily. She also has a cat named Jella.

- Kristen loves to read. Her favorite book is *East of Eden* by John Steinbeck.

- Kristen listens to big-band music and has taken swing dance classes.

Kristen filmed some of the scenes for *Panic Room* on the streets of New York City.

Key Events

From the age of nine, Kristen worked steadily as an actor. After playing Sarah Altman in *Panic Room*, Kristen began getting many more job offers.

In 2007, while filming a movie called *Adventureland*, Kristen received a phone call. It was from a movie **director** by the name of Catherine Hardwicke. Catherine's next project was a vampire movie called *Twilight*, which was based on a series of books by Stephenie Meyer. She wanted Kristen to audition for her.

Kristen had minutes to learn her lines, but her performance impressed Catherine. She was cast as Isabella "Bella" Swan in the movie. *Twilight* made $70.55 million in its first weekend. This was one of the most successful openings for an **independent film**.

Kristen's performance as Bella received good reviews and brought her many fans. In 2009, she won the MTV Movie Award for Best Female Performance. That same year, Kristen returned to the role of Bella Swan in the *Twilight* sequel *New Moon*. The second movie in the series was even more successful than the first.

◼ Kristen and other members of the Twilight cast often promote the movies together.

Thoughts from Kristen

Kristen has worked hard to become a successful actor. Here are some comments she has made about her movie roles and acting.

Kristen talks about being grateful for Twilight's success.

"I'm really proud of Twilight. I think it's a good movie. It was hard to do, and I think it turned out pretty good."

Kristen talks about her role as Bella Swan.

"I don't envy her, because it would be one of the most difficult positions to be in ever."

Kristen loves acting even though she does not like being in the spotlight.

"It's a little weird, but it's all because of this .... The focus for us is the focus that [the fans] have, which is the movies ... This is what you work for. Not the attention, but the fact that you can have a common interest."

Kristen talks about how her character changes in the Twilight movies.

"Each time, my character Bella became a different person, and I got to know that person and take her to the next level."

Kristen talks about her parent's support for her career choice.

"... they support anything that me and my brothers want to do. It was something I thought was fun because I grew up on sets."

Kristen loves acting.

"I would do it for free every day [even] if nobody saw it. I cannot describe how good it feels to actually have something that is truly into your heart and soul actually affecting people. And that's amazing."

What Is an Actor?

Actors are people that take on the roles of characters in theatrical productions. Stage, radio, television, and film all provide opportunities for actors to perform. Actors work long hours. Many actors train at acting schools or work with a drama coach to improve their skills.

Often, actors learn lines and movements that are written in scripts. Sometimes, actors do not use a script. They say and do what they feel in the moment. This is called improvisation.

In order to play different roles, actors need talent and experience. Skills such as dancing, singing, or athletics are often used to make a character more realistic. Some actors, such as Kristen Stewart, have other talents. Kristen enjoys singing and can play the guitar. She has used these musical skills in some of her roles. In the movie, *Into the Wild*, she sang in front of a crowd for the first time. For her role in *The Runaways*, Kristen was required to act and sing like rock icon Joan Jett.

■ Kristen and Joan Jett appeared together at the opening of *The Runaways*.

Actors 101

Emma Watson (1990–)

Emma was born in Paris, France. As a child, she enjoyed acting in school productions. Emma's first movie role was as Hermione Granger in *Harry Potter and the Sorcerer's Stone* in 2001. She has gone on to star in all the Harry Potter sequels. Emma is a celebrity model for the high-end label Burberry. Currently, Emma is a college freshman at Brown University in Providence, Rhode Island.

Dakota Fanning (1994–)

Dakota was born in Conyers, Georgia. As a child, she performed in local productions. Her big break came when she was cast in the movie *I am Sam,* which starred Sean Penn and Michelle Pfeiffer. She was nominated for a Screen Actors Guild Award for her work in this movie. In 2009, Dakota was cast in the *Twilight* sequel, *New Moon.*

Selena Gomez (1992–)

Selena was born in Grand Prairie, Texas. She began her television career on *Barney & Friends* playing Gianna for two years. She is best known for her role as Alex Russo on *Wizards of Waverly Place.* In 2008, Selena signed a music deal with Hollywood Records. The next year, she released her debut album *Kiss & Tell.* The same year, she co-starred with her friend and fellow actor Demi Lovato in the movie *Princess Protection Program.*

Demi Lovato (1992–)

Demi was born in Albuquerque, New Mexico. As a child, she starred in *Barney & Friends* with her friend, Selena Gomez. Years later, Demi starred with the Jonas Brothers in the Disney Channel movie *Camp Rock.* Besides acting, Demi is also a songwriter and singer. Her first album, *Don't Forget,* peaked at number two on the **Billboard** charts. Her second album, *Here We Go Again,* debuted at number one on the Billboard charts.

Moviemaking

Writers, directors, producers, crewmembers, actors, and editors work hard to make movies. They can take months, or even years, to create. Movies have been made in the United States since the early 1900s. The first movies were called silent films because they did not have sound.

Influences

Kristen has a strong relationship with her parents, and they have been a major influence in her life. Kristen has said she would like to attend university in Australia, where her mother was born.

Working with some of the best actors in the world has influenced Kristen. In *Into the Wild*, she was directed by Sean Penn. Working with Sean taught her a different creative process. He gave the actors confidence to take risks in their work.

■ *Into the Wild* landed Sean a nomination at the 2007 Director's Guild of America Awards.

Jodie Foster, Kristen's co-star in *Panic Room*, is another actor Kristen admires. Jodie has had a long career in Hollywood. She started as a child actor in the 1960s, and has since become a director, producer, and writer as well. Kristen has said that, like Jodie, she hopes to someday take on different jobs in the entertainment industry.

JULES MANN-STEWART

Kristen lives in Los Angeles. She splits her time between her own home and her family home. She is close to her mother, Jules Mann-Stewart. Kristen and her mother are currently working on a film together entitled *K-11*. The movie is set in a Los Angeles jail. Kristen's mother will be directing the movie. Fellow *Twilight* cast member Nikki Reed will star in the movie with Kristen.

■ Kristen and *Twilight* castmate Nikki Reed attended the film's world premiere in 2008.

Overcoming Obstacles

The stress of managing an acting career and school were difficult for Kristen. After grade seven, she left public school. She was then homeschooled using an online school. Kristen found online learning more flexible for her filming schedule. It also required her to be **disciplined**. It was too easy to fall behind on assignments if she did not study regularly.

When Kristen took the role of Bella Swan in *Twilight*, she did not know the movie was going to be so successful. She was unaware of fans' expectations for the film. With the movie's success, Kristen's life changed dramatically. She became known around the world.

■ Kristen Stewart's fame has made her a target for photographers.

At first, Kristen was overwhelmed. People wanted to know more about her. Cars and photographers waited outside her home daily. While filming *New Moon*, photographers camped outside of her hotel.

Thanks to the success of the Twilight movies, a great deal of attention is focused on Kristen's daily life. This has taught Kristen to be cautious when giving interviews and appearing in public. Even so, Kristen is grateful for the role of Bella. The role has given her a higher status as an actor.

■ Many of Kristen's fans have created websites with facts and photographs related to the actress.

Achievements and Successes

Kristen graduated from high school while filming the third Twilight movie, *Eclipse*. It was a great achievement for the busy actor. A picture was taken on the movie set of Kristen in her cap and gown, receiving her diploma, dressed as Bella.

The release of *Twilight* in 2008 was a surprise success. The movie made more than $380 million worldwide. Its sequel, *New Moon*, had the largest opening day sales in the United States of any movie to date, earning almost $75 million.

Kristen's acting career was in motion long before the Twilight movies, however. She had already received good reviews for her acting ability in other projects. In fact, Kristen has been **nominated** for a Young Artist Award four times. One nomination occurred in 2002 for her role in *Panic Room*. Another was for *Into the Wild*.

■ Kristen Stewart won the Orange Rising Star Award at the Orange British Academy Film Awards in 2010.

The Twilight movies have brought Kristen more praise. Following the release of the first movie in the series, *Entertainment Weekly* named Kristen one of the top 30 actresses under 30 years of age. *Vanity Fair* magazine named her one of Hollywood's "New Wave" of actors. In 2009, she was awarded the Teen Choice award for Movie Actress in a Drama and the MTV Movie award for Best Female Performance. In 2010, she won the People's Choice award for Favorite On-screen Team, along with her Twilight saga co-stars Robert Pattinson and Taylor Lautner. She has had many other award nominations as well.

HELPING OTHERS

Often, actors use their popularity to increase public awareness. They may bring attention to nonprofit organizations, environmental issues, or help fund special causes. Kristen is involved with several charities, including Walk to Cure Diabetes. Along with boxer Sugar Ray Leonard, Kristen served as a celebrity walk **ambassador** for the Juvenile Diabetes Research Foundation at their 2009 event. The walk drew about 15,000 supporters. To learn more about juvenile diabetes and the Walk To Cure Diabetes, visit **www.jdrf.org**.

Write a Biography

A person's life story can be the subject of a book. This kind of book is called a biography. Biographies describe the lives of remarkable people, such as those who have achieved great success or have done important things to help others. These people may be alive today, or they may have lived many years ago. Reading a biography can help you learn more about a remarkable person.

At school you might be asked to write a biography. First, decide whom you want to write about. You can choose a actor, such as Kristen Stewart, or any other person you find interesting. Then, find out if your library has any books about this person.

Learn as much as you can about him or her. Write down the key events in the person's life. What was this person's childhood like? What has he or she accomplished? What are his or her goals? What makes this person special or unusual?

A concept web is a useful research tool. Read the questions in the following concept web. Answer the questions in your notebook. Your answers will help you write your biography.

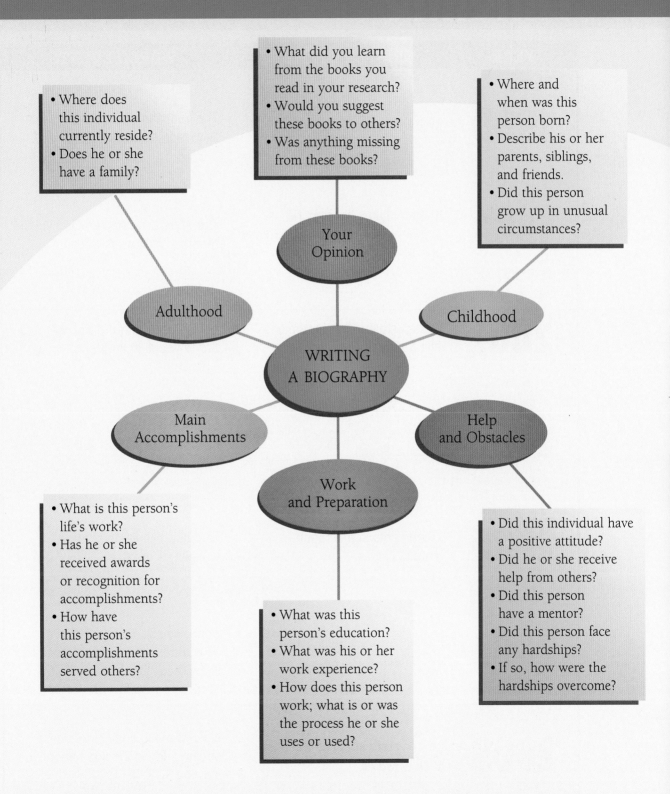

- Where does this individual currently reside?
- Does he or she have a family?

- What did you learn from the books you read in your research?
- Would you suggest these books to others?
- Was anything missing from these books?

- Where and when was this person born?
- Describe his or her parents, siblings, and friends.
- Did this person grow up in unusual circumstances?

Your Opinion

Adulthood

Childhood

WRITING A BIOGRAPHY

Main Accomplishments

Help and Obstacles

Work and Preparation

- What is this person's life's work?
- Has he or she received awards or recognition for accomplishments?
- How have this person's accomplishments served others?

- What was this person's education?
- What was his or her work experience?
- How does this person work; what is or was the process he or she uses or used?

- Did this individual have a positive attitude?
- Did he or she receive help from others?
- Did this person have a mentor?
- Did this person face any hardships?
- If so, how were the hardships overcome?

Timeline

YEAR	KRISTEN STEWART	WORLD EVENTS
1990	Kristen Stewart is born.	The Simpsons debuts on the Fox television network.
1999	Kristen makes her first TV appearance in the Disney Channel production *Thirteenth Year*.	The TiVo, a personal digital video recorder, makes its debut.
2001	Kristen stars in her first movie, *The Safety of Objects*.	*Harry Potter and the Sorcerer's Stone* opens in theaters.
2002	Kristen stars opposite Jodie Foster in *Panic Room*.	*Spider-Man* becomes the first film to make $100 million in its first three days.
2005	Kristen acts in the space fantasy *Zathura*.	YouTube, the video sharing website, is created.
2008	Kristen stars as Bella Swan in *Twilight*.	*High School Musical 3: Senior Year* breaks the opening weekend sales record for a musical.
2009	Kristen stars again as Bella Swan in *New Moon*.	*New Moon* has the single best opening day in cinema history, earning $72.7 million.

Words to Know | Index

agent: a person that finds talent for the entertainment industry and helps talent find jobs that suit their skills

ambassador: a representative

auditions: trial viewings of performers under consideration for a job

Billboard: charts produced by a weekly magazine that rate the popularity of music

director: a person who supervises the creative aspects of a dramatic production or film and instructs the actors and crew

disciplined: focused on a task

independent film: a movie produced without the funding or input of a major studio

nominated: recommended for an award

producer: a person who supervises the business of making a film

professional: someone who earns money for the work they do

script supervisor: a person on a movie set who maintains the consistency of the film

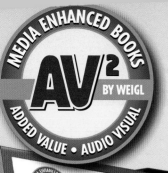

Log on to www.av2books.com

AV² by Weigl brings you media enhanced books that support active learning. Go to **www.av2books.com**, and enter the special code inside the front cover of this book. You will gain access to enriched and enhanced content that supplements and complements this book. Content includes video, audio, web links, quizzes, a slide show, and activities.

Audio
Listen to sections of the book read aloud.

Video
Watch informative video clips.

Web Link
Find research sites and play interactive games.

Try This!
Complete activities and hands-on experiments.

WHAT'S ONLINE?

 Try This!
Complete activities and hands-on experiments.

 Web Link
Find research sites and play interactive games.

 Video
Watch informative video clips.

EXTRA FEATURES

Pages 6-7 Complete an activity about your childhood.

Pages 10-11 Try this activity about key events.

Pages 16-17 Complete an activity about overcoming obstacles.

Pages 20-21 Write a biography.

Page 22 Try this timeline activity.

Pages 8-9 Learn more about Kristen Stewart's life.

Pages 14-15 Find out more about the people who influenced Kristen Stewart.

Pages 18-19 Learn more about Kristen Stewart's achievements.

Pages 20-21 Check out this site about Kristen Stewart.

Pages 4-5 Watch a video about Kristen Stewart.

Pages 12-13 Check out a video about Kristen Stewart.

Audio
Hear introductory audio at the top of every page.

Key Words
Study vocabulary, and play a matching word game.

Slide Show
View images and captions, and try a writing activity.

AV² Quiz
Take this quiz to test your knowledge

Due to the dynamic nature of the Internet, some of the URLs and activities provided as part of AV² by Weigl may have changed or ceased to exist. AV² by Weigl accepts no responsibility for any such changes. All media enhanced books are regularly monitored to update addresses and sites in a timely manner. Contact AV² by Weigl at 1-866-649-3445 or av2books@weigl.com with any questions, comments, or feedback.